GRAB MY HAND

As I Walk You Through The Homeowner Process

A Resource Guide For
First-Time Homebuyers

Copyright © 2022 by Davielier Turner

All rights reserved.

No part of this book may be reproduced in any form or by any electronic or mechanical means, including information storage and retrieval systems, without written permission from the author, except for the use of brief quotations in a book review.

GRAB MY HAND

As I Walk You Through The Homeowner Process

A Resource Guide For
First-Time Homebuyers

DAVIELIER TURNER

Are you a first-time homebuyer trying to figure out how to get started with the home buying process? Are you curious about how to finally get started to own a home of your own? Well, let this book guide you into taking the first leap into homeownership. This first-time homebuyer's guide is simple and to the point. Let it be a tool to guide you into your first home purchase.

CONTENTS

Introduction	ix
First Time Homeowner Process *Who's A First-Time Homeowner?*	1
Step 1 *What kind of home best meets your needs?*	5
Step 2 *What Specific Features Do You Want In Your Ideal Home?*	9
Step 3 *Getting To The Pre-Approval Process*	13
Step 4 *Preapproved And Knowing What You Can Afford*	23
Step 5 *Finding The Right Real Estate Agent Who Will Assist You And Guide You Through The Buying Process?*	29
Step 6 *Start Shopping for Your House and Make Offers*	35
Step 7 *Your Offer has been Accepted, What's Next? Attorney Review*	41
Step 8 *Get the Home Inspection*	45
Step 9 *Working with your Mortgage Rep to select Your Loan*	49
Step 10 *The Mortgage Commitment Is In Whats Next*	55
Step 11 *What is Title Insurance?*	59

Step 12 *What Does a Title Company Charge?*	63
Step 13 *When Do You Meet with the Title Company and How Often?*	67
Step 14 *Other Things That Must Be Done While Awaiting Title To Come Back*	71
Step 15 *Cleared To Close Now What*	75
You Are Now A Homeowner	81
Bonus Information	83
About the Author	85

INTRODUCTION

Getting to the mindset of finally deciding to become a homeowner has never been an easy task, as there are pros and cons to owning property.

Pros: tax write-offs, peace of mind to do and paint the walls whatever color you want in your house, children can be as loud as they want, or you can even play your weekend clean-up music as loud as you want to play it without anyone complaining. You don't have a fear of having to move because the landlord has sold or lost the house and didn't tell you until the last minute.

Cons: If something breaks, you are responsible for fixing it. There is no calling the owner for repair because you are the owner. Hence, you must keep funds aside should anything go wrong. If you look at the shortlist, the pros really do outweigh the cons of homeownership. The question here is, why are you still renting when it is clearly better to own your own property?

Did you know that the cost of owning is actually cheaper than the cost of renting? In the history of homeownership, the housing market crashes every 10-15 years or so, give or take, but one thing that never crashes is the rent price. When the market crash, it creates a demand for displaced homeowners, increasing rental amounts. When the market is good, housing costs more for homeowners to buy, creating higher rents. When you think about it, rent never goes down, and the renter is the one left paying the hefty rental price tag while they still do not own anything. Are you tired of getting nothing for the hundreds of thousands of rental incomes that you have put in someone else pocket?

In this book, we will go through the steps of making you a successful homeowner as you shall get ready and be prepared for homeownership.

But before we get started, the first thing and the most important thing that we need to do is to know where we stand with our credit. You can get a free credit report once a year from

www.freecreditreport.com

INTRODUCTION xi

www.Experian.com
www.Creditkarma.com

This is your most important step because, in order to think about getting a house, your credit must be in good condition. So, let's go online and register for the free reports so that we will know where we stand before we even get started.

The ache for a home lives in all of us, the safe place where we can go as we are and not be questioned.

MAYA ANGELOU

FIRST TIME HOMEOWNER PROCESS

WHO'S A FIRST-TIME HOMEOWNER?

A first-time homeowner is someone who hasn't owned a principal residence for the past three-year period ending on the date of acquisition of the new home—an individual that has no way possessed a property. Even if their partner was a homeowner already, the two may purchase together as first-time homebuyers.

The U.S. Department of Housing and City Development (HUD) established criteria to help distinguish first-time homebuyers for Federal Housing Administration (FHA) loan programs. A first-time homebuyer is an individual who meets any of the following criteria.

An individual that has not held power in a property during the three-time period ending on the date of the purchase.

For couples, if one mate is/was a homeowner, but the other has not held a home, both consorts are considered first-time homebuyers.

A single parent who has only held a home with a former mate while wedded is considered a first-time homebuyer.

Any person who is a displaced mate (has worked only in the home for a substantial number of times furnishing overdue ménage services for family members) and has only held a home with a mate is considered a first-time homebuyer.

A person that has only possessed a home that isn't permanently fixed to an endless foundation in agreement with applicable regulations (a mobile home).

The benefit to qualifying as a first-time homebuyer is access to programs offered through Federal Housing Administration (FHA). Programs can include low mortgage rates, low down payment, low ending costs, and loans for lower credit scores than needed for conventional (non-FHA) loans.

Finding a home, receiving finance, making an offer, getting a home inspection, and closing on the purchase are steps in the buying process. It's critical to maintain your property and save money once you've moved in.

If I were asked to name the chief benefit of the house, I should say: the house shelters daydreaming, the house protects the dreamer, the house allows one to dream in peace.

GASTON BACHELARD

STEP 1

WHAT KIND OF HOME BEST MEETS YOUR NEEDS?

Considerations Before You Buy a House

You have several options when copping a domestic property, a traditional single-family home, a townhouse, a condominium, or a multifamily construction with two to four units. Depending on your level of homeownership, each choice has advantages and disadvantages.

It's up to you to decide which type of property will help you become a comfortable homeowner. In any case, you can save money on the purchasing price by choosing a fixer-upper (although the quantum of time, sweat equity, and patience involved to turn a fixer-upper into your dream home might be much further than you bargained for).

Single-Family: is great for those who do not need rental assistance to pay for it or someone who just doesn't like people and does not even want to deal with any tenants.

Townhouse or Condo: Is great for a person that just want a place for themselves but with amenities (pool, gym, rec area). Also great for a person who does not want to be bothered with cutting grass or shoveling snow because you will pay an association fee that will most likely handle those things for you.

Multifamily dwelling 2-4 units: Great for an investor to start building a rental portfolio as you can live in one of the units and rent the others and gain rental income from the property. If you can live in one unit for free or at a discount as the others pay for your expenses, then that is the ultimate multifamily goal. Now you can save your money to purchase an additional rental property in the future if that is your goal.

You can't have everything you want, but you can have the things that really matter to you.

MARISSA MAYER

STEP 2
WHAT SPECIFIC FEATURES DO YOU WANT IN YOUR IDEAL HOME?

While it's good to have some inflexibility in this list, remember that you are making maybe the biggest purchase of your life; you earned the right to have that purchase fit both your requirements and wants as nearly as possible. You also must have flexibility because all the wants and needs are not always addressed in the house you purchase unless you have a big budget and can build it yourself. Creating a list of what's the most important must-haves will help you a lot. Your list should include introductory solicitations, like the neighborhood, school systems, and property size, all the way down to lower details like the number of restrooms, placement of the restrooms, and a kitchen that comes with the installed appliances. Real estate websites can be a precious tool for probing parcels that satisfy your solicitations and conditions for your new home. Also, one of the biggest mistakes new homeowners make is they do not believe in starter houses. Remember, your first home might not be your forever home, so it's ok not to get everything that you want the first purchase as there will be more years to gain more income and get the dream home that you really desire. Also, one must truly understand their budget with today's market so that it will really align with your wants and needs. Price points will really determine how much house you can afford and if it's realistic to get all the things that you want within your budget for your first home. Do market research so that you can see what houses are going for today. You can scroll through Realtor.com, Trulia, Zillow, or any homeowner website to get a good idea.

Once you're a homeowner, your house will probably be the biggest, long-term investment you have. Every dollar you spend on a mortgage or down payment is like putting money in a house-sized piggy bank, so it makes sense to look at home buying through the lens of saving.

RACHEL CRUZE

STEP 3
GETTING TO THE PRE-APPROVAL PROCESS

Before you start looking for a home, you need to figure out how much a lender is willing to lend you to buy your first home. You may suppose you can go as high as you want in price, but lenders may suppose you are only good for a certain amount, depending on factors like how much other debt you have, your yearly income, and the length of time you've been at your current position. These are very important factors in the qualifying process.

Before getting your hopes up to purchase and or contacting a realtor to show you houses, be sure you're pre-approved for financing. In numerous cases, sellers will not indeed entertain an offer that's not accompanied by a mortgage pre-approval. In addition, numerous realtors do not spend time with buyers who have not been preapproved by a mortgage broker, banker, credit union or a bank. Begin by probing lenders and comparing interest rates. Also, submit your application for a mortgage and include the supporting paperwork requested by your lender to justify your income and debt.

Lenders will ask for the following to get started:

1. Last two years of tax returns plus your 1099/w2 forms.
2. Last 2/3 months of bank statements from all accounts (bank, retirement, IRA, 401k).
3. A legit copy of your social security card.
4. Last 2 Months of pay stubs
5. A copy of your valid and up-to-date driver's license and/or passport.

If a lender does not ask for all of these and just checks your credit and gives you a pre-approval letter, be very wary. Those are the types of lenders that will later say that you do not qualify because they have not seen all your documents yet. Ensure a lender checks everything before they give you a purchase amount. Make sure the lender explains the complete loan process to you, so there are no surprises later. Also, have the lender break down the costs of the different items that you will pay for, such as appraisal, prepaid taxes, origination fee, and other items that you will be paying for with your loan and closing costs. Most lenders will inflate the costs so that there is no surprise later and you will end up paying less. You never have to argue with a buyer that's paying less than what they were quoted, but they will definitely have to argue and explain how they got to the higher costs of lending.

The good thing about residential real estate is that you can purchase with little or no money down. And the reason is most loans are government-backed. FHA, VA, and conventional are all government-backed loans. Some require private mortgage insurance (PMI); some say mortgage insurance premium (MIP). VA is backed by the government through the department of veteran affairs. They back and assist first-time homeowners.

FHA Loan — 3.5% down

FHA loans - loans backed by the federal government and intended for homebuyers who are usually not qualified for a conventional mortgage by allowing lower down payment.

Conventional Loan — 3%-20% down (varies)

Conventional loans - a loan that's not backed by the government and guaranteed to the private sector. It is one of the most used.

VA Loan — 0% down for Veterans (Thank you for your service)

VA loan- housing loan backed by the Department of Veterans Affairs for those who have served or currently serve in the US military.

These government-backed loans make it easier for first-time homeowners to purchase a place to call home.

One more thing about residential real estate.

Condos and co-ops have additional maintenance fees. Some are FHA-approved, and some are not. If a condo is not FHA-approved, then you might have to go conventional and put a higher down payment down because the building or the management company did not meet the requirements for the property to be on the FHA-approved list. (Make sure that your loan officer gets in-depth with these scenarios because all are crucial to what time of property that you will be purchasing.

Also, inquire with your loan officer about (DPA) down payment assistance programs because there are a lot of government back programs. Some loan officers know about them while some do not, so do your research as well and come ready with the questions for them during the pre-approval process.

Additional costs associated with your loan that your loan officer shall explain. So make sure some of these costs are noted upfront so you will have enough funds at closing time to close the deal.

1. Application
2. Appraisal Fee
3. Attorney Fee
4. Escrow Fee
5. Courier Fee
6. Credit Report
7. Flood Determination

8. Home Inspection
9. Homeowner's Insurance
10. Underwriting Fee
11. Lenders Policy Title insurance
12. Origination Fee
13. Prepaid Interest
14. Private Mortgage Insurance
15. Property Tax
16. Recording Fee
17. Survey Fee
18. Exam Fee
19. Transfer Fee
20. VA Funding Fee

Typical home buyers will pay between 3%-5% of the purchase price in closing fees. Your Loan Officer and/or Attorney will break most of these costs down to you.

Your monthly rent or mortgage payment should be no more than 25% of your take-home pay. Take-home pay is your income after taxes have been taken out.

When it comes to a mortgage, my suggested 25% limit includes the principal, interest, taxes, and insurance, along with any monthly HOA fees.

A lot of people will be upset by this advice, but you don't get a pass on math because of where you live. I've seen people do a lot of stupid stuff with real estate, and I don't want you to be house poor.

If you don't make enough to live in an area where the real estate is expensive, that means you don't make enough to live in an area where the real estate is expensive, and that's **OKAY**. One day your math may look different, but if you're trying to fudge the numbers now, you'll regret it later when you have too many months left at the end of your money. Don't hurt yourself financially because you feel like you've got to try to keep up.

There are a **LOT** of real estate agents looking for a higher commission and a lot of mortgage companies looking to lend you **WAY** more than what I'm advising. Don't take their word for it. Just because they're willing to lend you a high amount doesn't mean that's how much you should borrow. Do your own math and think about this in detail. I want you to own your home, **NOT** let your home own you. You need the other 75% of your take-home pay to cover the other areas of your budget and make progress toward your future. Owning your home and getting it paid off is a vital part of having a successful financial future.

Land monopoly is not only monopoly, but it is by far the greatest of monopolies; it is a perpetual monopoly, and it is the mother of all other forms of monopoly.

WINSTON CHURCHILL

STEP 4

PREAPPROVED AND KNOWING WHAT YOU CAN AFFORD

On the other hand, occasionally and only if you qualify, a bank will give you a loan approval for more houses than you really want to pay for. Just because a bank says it'll approve you for a certain amount of dollars doesn't mean you should spend that much. Numerous first-time homebuyers make this mistake and end up being what's called "house-poor" — meaning after they pay their monthly mortgage payment, they have no finances left over for other costs, such as clothes, date night, childcare expenses, entertainment, or indeed food.

When considering how much of a loan to take out, you will want to look at the house's total cost, not just the monthly payment. Consider how high the property taxes are in your chosen neighborhood, the cost of your homeowner's insurance, and the monthly water bill amount. How much do you need saved to maintain the upkeep of the house in case of emergency, for example, the furnace or water tank breaks down, the stove goes out, or the water main breaks? Any of these things can, and I might say, will eventually happen.

One must really understand the hidden costs of homeownership in order to maintain it.

1. Property Taxes
2. Homeowner's Insurance
3. HOA (Homeowner Association Fee Condo/Co-op)
4. Roof
5. Lawn Care
6. Plumbing
7. Pest Control
8. Electrical System
9. Heating/Ventilation/Air-Conditioning

Certain home warranties are good to invest in too. North Jersey Public Service Electric & Gas has a program called WorryFree. They charge monthly on your bill per appliance, and you can protect your furnace, water heater, refrigerator, dishwasher, washer machine & dryer, all of those for about an extra $35 a month. It sounds like a lot when counting bills, but look at it like as one washing machine repair can cost up to $400 to repair without a warranty. The only thing is if they can't repair it, then they do not pay for the replacement. But with respect to the contract, they will fix it as many times as possible until they cannot repair it anymore, and then it is dead, and you will have to purchase a new one. I remember I had a huge house in East Orange, NJ, and the central air & heat unit used to go out at least four times a year, and I refused to replace it, and they came and fixed it every time, so it was definitely a plus for me to have that service. Another good warranty service to get is the water main service from your house to the street. We never know when the main sewer line can bust, clog or anything. They sell these services, but a job like that can easily run about $8000 to $20,000 depending on the company that you pick to "ROB" you less for the repair.

Typically, the research tells us that a high-quality real estate agent that really knows what they are doing will add more to the equation than they cost

STEP 5

FINDING THE RIGHT REAL ESTATE AGENT WHO WILL ASSIST YOU AND GUIDE YOU THROUGH THE BUYING PROCESS?

Once you are preapproved, it is up to you to do your due diligence to find the best real estate agent that can help you find your home. A real estate agent will help you locate homes that meet your requirements and are in your price range, they will research the area of your liking, and they will send houses to you by text or email daily. It is also up to you to search online and see if you find a house and send it to them to get you in to see it. They'll meet with you to show you the houses that you both agree that you want to see. Typically, a realtor will pick out a few more places they believe may be a right fit for you than you have seen pictures for.

The agent can be an experienced agent or a new agent. Some will say get an experienced agent, but I will say find an agent that's willing to work for you. Some experienced agents have become lazy, while some newer agents are firecrackers and ready to help you get to the closing table because they are hungry. These professionals can assist you in negotiating the entire buying process, including making an offer, obtaining financing if you have not obtained it yet, and completing paperwork once you've decided on a home to buy.

A good real estate agent's experience can assist you in taking serious risks you might encounter during the process, as most will direct you in the best way to get you to the finish line of homeownership with the proper care and professionalism. Agents get paid a commission that is paid from the seller's proceeds. Although they are working for you, the seller still pays them, so the best thing a client can do is give an agent their loyalty as the agent shall return the same through the process. Some agents will also ask that you sign a buyer's agency agreement stating that they will work for you, and if you go anywhere, they can charge you a fee. There is a saying in real estate that "buyers are liars." This does not hold true for all, but for some, this is a simple direct truth not based on hearsay but based on experience. Some agents like to protect their time and the gas that they use showing a buyer property and they are only trying to lock in your loyalty. Time is very important to an agent, so please be sure that homeownership is what you really want and that you are not treading the line. We know things do happen and force people to push back their search until another time, so we understand that. Just make sure ownership is what you want because an agent does not make one dime on a sale until you close the property. So please just think and be considerate by not having an agent show you 60 houses in 4 months before deciding you never really wanted a house. My personnel theory is that 60% of homeowners are sure that they want a house, 30% want to walk the fence, and the other 10% just be wasting time. The more serious you are in your search, the more intentional the agent becomes by wanting to find that smile on your face and getting you to your dream. I found that the clients that are looking online and sending you houses as well are the most serious customers because they are working with you and showing their sincerity. Once again, an agent and a client can become the best of friends when they are working together for a common goal; that's why it's very important to find the right agent for your search.

Buyers decide in the first eight seconds of seeing a home if they're interested in buying it.

UNKNOWN

STEP 6

START SHOPPING FOR YOUR HOUSE AND MAKE OFFERS

Look at homes in your price range. Make sure that you are comfortable with a price range and monthly payment amount. It might be helpful to take notes on all the homes you visit. Go to the open houses and research online. You will see a lot of houses. Some great, some good, and plenty bad, but with potential. It can be hard to recollect everything about them, so you might want to take plenty of pictures and videos to help you recollect each home. This process is not easy because one day you like a house, and the next day there might be another that you like or you might put an offer in for one and then see one with more of the features that you wanted. Knowing what's the most important of your wants and needs is very critical for shopping because no one ever really gets everything they want in a house unless they build it themselves, so knowing your must-haves and what you can live without is very important.

Once you find something you like, the agent will write it up, have you sign it, then send it over to the other agent and keep their fingers crossed that they accept your offer. At the time of writing this book, we are in a very competitive sellers' market here in New Jersey, so some offers are at the asking price and most of them are over the asking price. Putting in the right offer at the right time will determine if the client accepts your offer. When submitting an offer, the best thing you can ask yourself is, "If this was your house, what offer would you want and expect?" I say this to say a lowball offer might not get a counteroffer sent back to the agent and a seller can feel disrespected with a lowball offer that they might not even respond to your offer. Making your offer is based on your agent knowing the market and the location. Once you hire an agent, trust their judgment. Do not be the one saying my parents purchased a house 20 years ago and they said that I should offer this amount. In the 2022 saying of the rapper Fat Joe, "Today's price isn't yesterday's price." This is very true because listening to family and friends can have you lose out on a house that you really want. Once you and the agent connect on a house you like, that realtor will write it up, send it to the other agent (listing agent), and hope that it gets accepted.

If your offer does get accepted, the next part of the process will start. But this market is different, so you might get accepted quickly or let down quickly too. Be prepared to continue house searching just in case. Please make sure that the offer you submit is competitive. Most houses are going at the asking price or above. Don't be afraid to shoot your shot because, during the next phase, your attorney can do what's next to protect you.

Find out where the people are going and buy the land before they get there.

WILLIAM PENN ADAIR

STEP 7

YOUR OFFER HAS BEEN ACCEPTED, WHAT'S NEXT? ATTORNEY REVIEW

The next part is one of the most important and time crucial parts. You go into what is called an "Attorney Review Period." Although in certain places, attorneys are replaced with title company reps, in North Jersey, an attorney is highly suggested as should anything go wrong, they know who to blame and sue. This Is where the seller's attorney and the buyer's attorney will go back in forth about the things in the contract while they both of them work it out on each of their client's behalf. You will see notations with agree/disagree on the contract because this is them protecting your best interest and working for the fee that you pay them to protect you. Some attorneys will ask for their fee upfront. This is a security policy as in case the deal does not go through or close, they have been paid.

For most deals that do fall or do not close, the attorney may or may not ask you for the full fee for the next deal you bring to them to close for you. Some will ask for a portion of what's referred to as a deposit. This is to make sure that you are serious as they do not work for free either. When attorneys know you have no problem paying and are serious, they tend to work harder for you too, and some will ask for it at closing, and it will be on the hud1/closing disclosure statement (paperwork stating that you closed on the house). No matter which way you look at it, they will be collecting their payment. They will go back and forth until this review is done, and only when it's done do you have a legal and binding contract. If another offer happens to come in during this time to the seller, the seller can have the option to entertain it. Hence, it is very important to get out of the attorney review as soon as possible because you can lose the deal. Once they have agreed, then your next phase shall begin.

Also, at this time, the agent will have sent a copy of the contract to your loan officer as they will be awaiting confirmation from your attorney that the review is over so that they may order their appraisal and get the file processed by underwriting.

Don't beat yourself up. Some transactions will naturally go smoothly, and others are a month of challenges.

UNKNOWN

STEP 8
GET THE HOME INSPECTION

Generally, purchase offers are contingent on a home inspection of the property to check for signs of structural damage or effects that may need fixing. Your real estate agent generally will help you arrange to have this inspection conducted within ten days of your offer being received and accepted by the Seller, as well as attorney review being concluded. This inspection protects you by giving you a chance to keep your offer, negotiate with the seller about the repairs or withdraw it without penalty if the inspection reveals any significant material damage.

Both you and the Seller will submit a report on the home inspector's findings. You can also decide if you want to ask the seller to fix anything on the property or you can ask for a seller concession to do any repairs yourself to ensure that they are done correctly before closing. If you agree to let the seller do the repairs before the closing, you'll have a walkthrough of the house, which gives you the chance to validate that any agreed-upon repairs have been made and done correctly. The main things you want to always look out for in a home inspection are as follows

1. Foundation problems
2. Anywhere that water can come in
3. Electrical issues
4. Roofing
5. Heating System
6. Plumbing
7. Termite damage

These are the biggest components when it comes to the inspection as these are the most expensive items to repair or replace. So, it is very wise to check reviews and hire an experienced professional to do the home inspection for you the right way. Please do not bring your cousin for cheap because he gave you a discount and he fixed a few items at the family house. I highly suggest hiring a licensed professional as it is in your best interest.

Consider a 15-year or a 20-year fixed rate instead of a 30-year, If you can afford the monthly payments. They might not be as high as you think.

SUZIE ORMAN

STEP 9

WORKING WITH YOUR MORTGAGE REP TO SELECT YOUR LOAN

Although you and the lender have spoken, and docs have already been submitted in order for them to get you the preapproval letter to search for homes. You will still have to meet with your loan officer to sign the mortgage application and all the disclosures that will be needed from you so that they may submit your loan to the underwriting process and get you approved to close the loan. Lenders have a wide range of aggressive-priced loan programs and a character for exceptional client service. You'll have numerous questions when you're copping a home and having one of our educated, responsive mortgage bankers help you can make the process much easier.

Every homebuyer has their own precedence when choosing a mortgage. Some are interested in keeping their yearly payments as low as possible. Others are focused on making sure that their yearly payments do not increase. And still, others pick a loan grounded on the knowledge they will be moving many times again. This is when you and your lender will go over what's for you and in your best interest with a fine-tooth comb. This is also where they will give you an estimate of monthly payments, tell you all the projected fees and smile while you are listening and feeling like you are being robbed. Your lender will order the appraisal next to determine the value of the property, and "yes," you will be paying for that too. They charge upfront for the appraisal with a credit or debit card. They will also discuss closing costs and all fees associated with this loan at this time and present you with what's called a good faith estimate.

The Good Faith Estimate, or GFE, is an extremely important document for potential homebuyers. Required by law to be provided within three days of your mortgage application, it is an estimate of the potential closing costs associated with a loan from a particular lender.

The fees included within a good faith estimate fall into six basic categories:

- Loan fees
- Fees to be paid in advance

- Reserves
- Title charges
- Government charges
- Additional charges

You will have a breakdown of all the fees associated with this loan.

Once the appraisal is done and comes back, your lender will give your attorney what is called a mortgage commitment outlining what other docs are needed from you and if the underwriter has approved you.

I don't have a muse. I have a mortgage.

JIM BUTCHER

STEP 10

THE MORTGAGE COMMITMENT IS IN WHATS NEXT

The next step is your attorney ordering title work on the property. The title company makes sure a property title is legitimate so that the buyer may be confident that once he buys a property, he is the rightful owner of the property. To ensure that the title is valid, the title company will do a title search, which is a thorough examination of property records to make sure that the person or company claiming to own the property does, in fact, legally own the property and that no one else could claim full or partial ownership of the property. The title insurance company also may be responsible for conducting the closing.

During the title search, the title company also looks for any outstanding mortgages, liens, judgments, or unpaid taxes associated with the property, as well as any restrictions, easements, leases, or other issues that might impact ownership. The title company may also require a property survey, which determines the boundaries of the plot of land that a home sits on, whether the home sits within those boundaries or have encroachments on the property by neighbors or any easements that may impact an ownership claim.

Before a title company issues title insurance, it will prepare an abstract of title, which is a short summary of what it found during the title search (basically, this is the history of the ownership of the property). Then, it will issue a title opinion letter, which is a legal document that speaks to the validity of the title.

Pessimists calculate the odds; Optimists believe they can overcome them

TED KOPPEL

STEP 11

WHAT IS TITLE INSURANCE?

Once the title is found to be valid, the title company will likely issue a title insurance policy, which protects lenders or owners against claims or legal fees that may arise from disputes over the ownership of the property.

There are two main types of title insurance: owner's title insurance, which protects the property owner from title issues, and lender's title insurance, which protects the mortgage company. You, the home buyer, will pay for the lender's title insurance when you close on the house, but it's also a good idea to make sure you have an owner's title insurance policy as well (in some areas of the country, sellers pay for these policies; in others, the buyer must purchase it).

For example, you buy a home and get both lenders and buyer's title insurance, but then someone comes forward claiming they are the rightful owner of the home. If, in fact, the title was wrong and they are the rightful owner of the home, your title insurance policy will likely pay you the value of the home and the lender the amount they lent you to buy the home.

To me, job title does not matter. Everyone is in sales. It's the only way we stay in business.

HARVEY MACKAY

STEP 12

WHAT DOES A TITLE COMPANY CHARGE?

The cost of title insurance depends on the size of the loan and varies greatly depending on the state. The good news is that the premium is a one-time fee you pay at closing, not an ongoing expense.

According to the Federal Reserve, "a lender's policy on a $100,000 loan can range from $175 in one state to $900 in another." You'll typically pay an additional amount — usually a few hundred dollars or more, depending on the size of the loan and your state of residence — for a buyer's policy.

Note that you may be able to get a discounted rate on your title insurance if the property was sold within the previous five years; just call and ask.

Being smiled upon before being robbed is one of the most misleading acts.

UNKNOWN

STEP 13

WHEN DO YOU MEET WITH THE TITLE COMPANY AND HOW OFTEN?

You may meet with or talk to an agent from the title company on multiple occasions. First, you may decide to meet with a few agents from title companies before you buy your home to help you decide which company to go with.

If the title company maintains an escrow account for you, the agent may reach out to you to provide details on that account, or you may contact him with questions.

If your title company handles your closing, you will meet with a settlement agent in person then. At this time, the settlement agent will explain all the documents related to the settlement before you sign anything. And, of course, if something goes wrong with regards to the title, you will likely meet with one of their agents then.

Also, on the title, they can find out if you owe any past judgments, such as child support, old bail bonds or anything. There are times when people have similar names, and they will make you go through a list stating if any judgments are yours or not.

Once the title is in and everything is satisfactory and clear, the attorney will submit it to your lender so that they can go over everything and get you prepared to close.

Real Estate is an imperishable asset, ever increasing in value. It is the most solid SECURITY that human ingenuity has devised. It is the basis of all security and the only indestructible security.

RUSSEL SAGE

STEP 14

OTHER THINGS THAT MUST BE DONE WHILE AWAITING TITLE TO COME BACK

There are also other things that must be done while the attorney is awaiting title report and underwriting clearance to close.

1. Most cities require a smoke certification. (Document stating they have inspected for smoke/carbon detectors and fire extinguisher on the premises)
2. CCC (Certificate Code Compliance) Certification stating that the city has inspected the premises and it has been approved to be used, or it will be given a temporary one stating that the buyer will be responsible for all of the repairs and that the property will be inspected again for the repairs at a later date.

3. Homeowner's Insurance must be purchased and paid for one year upfront. After that, the bank will escrow it with monthly payments and pay for it in the following years for you.

Once all of these are in, they will be submitted to your attorney and to your loan officer for clearance to close. The closing will usually be 2 to 3 days after the clear to close, but in some instances, they can close the same day or the next day if everyone is pushing to close at month's end or another situation arises (e.g., rate lock expire, time of the essence issued).

When the mortgage company comes back with the clear to close, they will let your attorney know and your attorney will set up a closing date with you and the seller's attorney.

Success in real estate starts when you believe that you are worthy of it.

MICHAEL FERRARA

STEP 15
CLEARED TO CLOSE NOW WHAT

Once underwriting issues the clear to close for your file, it will then be up to your attorney and your lender to coordinate the date and time for closing.

Once this is done, your designated real estate agent will set up a final walkthrough for the closing. As a professional real estate agent, I always suggest that the client do the walkthrough a few hours before closing. If you do it the night before and someone breaks in, you can be held responsible, so I always suggest the day of and right before the closing.

You will walk through and check all requested repairs, if any, to make sure they are corrected and in working order. Make sure the house is swept broom-clean so that you will not be responsible for cleaning out the house unless that is something that you agreed to. If there is anything wrong, take pictures and send them to your attorney before you get to closing so that they have a chance to work things out with the seller's attorney before you even get there.

The attorney or the title company will call you early or the night before and give you the numbers of how much money will be needed from your bank account to bring to the closing. All the funds must be submitted in the form of certified check; some accept it by wire transfer.

Once you get to the closing, your attorney, your agent, and you will be there. Sometimes, the seller and their attorney will come too, but lately, I have seen a lot of mail closings since the covid pandemic. You will see a packet and do not get scared because it might be the size of a phonebook. I hope that you took your arthritis pills because your signing hand will need it. If it's an FHA loan, you'll get a really thick package that would feel like you are signing forever. It will feel like you are signing your life away, and you are, but don't be afraid, it's not a deal with the devil, at least. Basically, what's in the package is saying that the house owns you for 30 years unless you sell it before then (LOL). Once all the documents are signed and your hand is in pain, the attorney or the title agent will fax over the signed docs to your lender. As soon as the lender replies that all the documents are good, guess what? The attorney will hand you your keys and

"CONGRATULATIONS, YOU ARE NOW A HOMEOWNER!"

You did it.

You have set out and completed your goal in homeownership.

If you don't own a home, buy one. If you own a home, buy another one. If you own two homes, buy a third.

JOHN PAULSON

YOU ARE NOW A HOMEOWNER

You have now made the biggest purchase of your life. Well, maybe, because student loans cost more than a house sometimes. But you have now made the biggest purchase of your life and have checked off the biggest task on your to-do list. You have conquered your fear, and now, you own a piece of the land that you pay taxes for. Although there are a lot of people that want to own a house, some of them can't, and many factors play into that. Some cannot do what you did to accomplish what you have accomplished. Now I want you to think about this; for the past few months, during this house process, you have learned to slow down on using your credit cards and minimize your spending and debt. You have learned to tell people no to co-signing, as well as control your bank account. Now apply this to everyday living from now on, and the next thing you know, you will own a few properties if that is indeed your goal. Congratulations, and thank you for taking this homeowner journey with me.

BONUS INFORMATION

THINGS NOT TO DO WHEN YOU ARE ABOUT TO SEARCH FOR A HOUSE

1. Do Not Purchase a Vehicle
2. Do not co-sign anything for anyone
3. Do not start purchasing furniture
4. Do not use your credit cards at all; it can affect your debt ratio
5. Do not place large deposits bigger than your paycheck in your account
6. Do not continuously transfer money through bank accounts
7. Do not remove money from your bank account
8. Do not be late on any payments
9. Do not let anyone pull your credit for anything

10. Do not apply for any new lines of credit at all

ABOUT THE AUTHOR

As a real estate agent with over 20 years of experience, I have taken parts of those 20+ years, good and bad, and put them in this book. I want people to see and understand that it is less difficult than it seems. This book is for experienced professionals, new agents, flippers, landlords, wholesalers, or anyone seeking simple information for their personal use. This book can be a guide to accomplish those goals as well as earn a profit.

Davielier Turner is an established real estate broker in the New Jersey area that has been selling, listing, and flipping real estate for over 20+ years. He is also part owner of Pinnacle Real Estate Group and the sole owner of B.C Enterprises, a company that specializes in flipping properties.

Made in the USA
Columbia, SC
07 June 2022